T0197141

EMPOWERING OUR KIDS... AND OURSELVES

THE QUOTESMEISTER TALKS TO HIS TWIN TEENS

by Richard Paul Hinkle

authorHOUSE

AuthorHouse™
1663 Liberty Drive
Bloomington, IN 47403
www.authorhouse.com
Phone: 833-262-8899

Published by AuthorHouse 12/30/2022

ISBN: 978-1-6655-7515-7 (sc)
ISBN: 978-1-6655-7517-1 (hc)
ISBN: 978-1-6655-7516-4 (e)

Library of Congress Control Number: 2022920803

Cover photo: The author with his not-yet-teen son, Curtis. Permission granted.

Print information available on the last page.

Dedicated to Beverly Jean Harris Hinkle,
Terry Lynn Salmon Abrams , Curtis William
Hinkle & Tamara Nicole Hinkle Leavitt.

CONTENTS

FOREWORD

I am a collector of quotes, as was my father before me. The idea of this book is simple enough: I collect quotes that heighten and focus life's meaning for myself, and I want to share these snippets of wisdom with my newly teenaged twins, Curtis William and Tamara Nicole. I want to give them the values and the guidance that these quotes embody. I know how much it eventually meant to me to hear my father's favorite ringing in my ears over the years: **"Never judge a man until you've walked a mile in his moccasins."** (I'm sure that my dad's love of this quote has at least something to do with the fact that we Hinkles are part Cherokee.)

As something of a self-taught philosopher—I wrote a "philosophy of life" newspaper column for nine years—I began collecting the quotes that follow. I have since added my own commentary so that Curt and Tama would have an enduring record of what I think it most important that they know and learn. (I later invited their reluctant comments, to thicken the soup, as it were.)

I hope this book will guide them, especially through their tough, hormone-enraged teens. I want them to attain their adulthood fully armed to deal with anything life can toss at them, from the simple allure of avoiding life via laziness and *ennui* on through the terrifying tragedy of escape by means of drugs or alcohol. I want them to feel so secure in their identities that no one and no idea could ever alter their innate senses of who they are and who they are becoming.

I am, as always, guided in this effort by a wonderfully

empowering quote from a Midwestern psychologist (as I understand him to be) by the name of Haim Ginott, who once counseled, **"Treat a child as though he already is the person he's capable of becoming."** [*Tamara: I like this quote because I hate it when people treat me like I'm still eight years old, when they treat me like I don't matter. It's sort of like a slap in the face.*] In a single word, that is respect. But it is more than that, too. It is also an acknowledgement to a child—who is at a point in life where any and all acknowledgement is precious beyond their means to fully express—that allows her to see something of herself that is so far into the future as to be nearly inexpressible. But when a child is allowed even a glimpse of that "possibility," he will run with it, and make of it far more than even we, with all our parental experience, can imagine. That is a most wondrous thing.

INTRODUCTION

An essential aspect of getting to the point of being fully empowered, fully armed lies in taking on the responsibility for your own lives, kids. Mark Twain had one take on that when he wrote, **"Don't go around saying the world owes you a living. The world owes you nothing. It was here first."** My father's take was that I could be anything I wanted to be . . . so long as I wasn't afraid to work my butt off for it.

As anyone familiar with George Bernard Shaw might expect, the magnificent British dramatist had a still pithier viewpoint on the subject: **"I don't believe in circumstances.**

The people who get on in this world are the people who get up and look for the circumstances they want, and, if they can't find them, make them.**" Whew! Talk about your self-starters. But there is an essential truth embedded and embodied by that admonition: If you create your own life, you own it. You choose whether it is to be forceful and commanding or fearful and cowering. Please, you two, opt for the former over the latter. It's a lot more rewarding.

Whenever you may be faced with a challenge—and it will happen often—recall the Chinese understanding of the concept of crisis, and what it really represents. As was taught me in my crisis hot-line training, the Chinese ideogram for "crisis" is constructed to two ideograms, one standing for "**danger**," the other for "**opportunity**." Always keep that in mind, that anything that challenges you also gives you that chance to grow. I believe Friedrich Nietzsche put it this way: "**That which does not kill you will make you stronger.**" [*Curtis: I love to get challenges, too, because it makes me smarter and better at different things.*]

One bit of guiding light that has always informed my decisions, and helped me to take a chance when I might not otherwise have done so, was a slender quip of advice accompanying a poster that was tacked onto the ceiling at San Francisco's Irwin Memorial Blood Bank. As you reclined on the donor's table, you saw a three-masted sailing ship, with all its canvas gloriously unfurled, the wind at her back. The caption was this: **"A ship in a harbor is safe, but that's not what ships are built for."** The meat of life goes to those willing to risk life, willing to put themselves to the test, and willing to face failure and success on equal terms. That's what truly *living* is all about. [*Curtis: I need to take more risks, because I'm scared that I might fail. I should think positive instead of negative thoughts.*]

One must know what one is about, of course, and be well focused on the direction in which one is headed. Observed Supreme Court jurist Oliver Wendell Holmes Jr., **"If you want to hit a bird on the wing, you must have all your will in a focus. You must not be thinking about** yourself, and, equally, you must not be thinking about your neighbor; you must be living in your eye on that bird. Every achievement is a bird on the wing."

It helps, of course, to understand that, no matter how motivated and how hard working and how focused you are, things are not always going to go your way. Here, a little of the Zen notion of unattachedness will go a long way. Focus more on the work and less on the goal would be one way of putting it. Novelist Alice Walker put it another way: "Expect nothing; live frugally on surprise." Will that work for you guys? I hope so.

HAVE CHARACTER, BE THE CHARACTER

Everything that is good and important about life begins with an individual's character. The single most important thing to learn about character is this: If you learn to be internally motivated and internally satisfied, you have armed yourself to take on the very worst that can be tossed at you by life.

So the first lesson is one of self-esteem, that inestimable, ineffable learning to be at one with your own self. In self-esteem seminars that I give to corporate clients I always begin with Eleanor Roosevelt's sagacious tidbit of wisdom, a comment that is so pithy, so dense with meaning that it could almost stand alone as a guideline for a life well-lived. Said Franklin Delano Roosevelt's ever-campaigning wife, "**No one can make you feel inferior without your consent**." [*Tamara: I totally agree. But for some people, it's hard to realize. I'm very emotional, and sometimes my emotions take control.*]

The essence is sound, powerful. You have the right, indeed the obligation (to yourself) to choose your response to anything, no matter how outrageous, no matter how vile, no matter how treacherous. At its most innocent, it is Lucy, having fallen on her roller skates, pointing to Charlie Brown, saying, "See what you made me do!" How many of us, in our childish (or worse, adult) *naïveté*, have ever bought into that bait, fallen for that social trap?

Here is the other extreme. A Cuban newspaper editor had just been released by Castro. He had been held in a Havana jail for ten or fifteen years. As he was descending the ramp from the airplane in Miami, reporters crowded around asking, "Do you hate Castro?" "Do you hate Cuba?" He paused, then replied, "No. Because if I did, it would mean that they still have some hold on me. They didn't have a hold on me when I was in their jail, and I'll be damned if they'll have a hold on me now that I'm not."

That is some serious withholding of consent, I don't care what anyone says. If you have the internal wherewithal to withstand the torturous, depraved conditions of unfair and inhumane imprisonment, you are armed to handle any and all of life's vicissitudes. Nelson Mandela's rise out of prison to become President of South Africa offers a parallel example.

So, too, was logotherapy founder Viktor E. Frankel, who survived the Nazis and Auschwitz. Wrote he, "**Everything can be taken from man but one thing: the last of human freedoms—to choose one's own attitude in any given set of circumstances, to choose one's own way.**" That, above all, is the lesson I want you two to garner from this small volume, the fact that you get to, *have to* choose your own lives. Never, never let anyone or anything else wrest that control from your hands, your minds, your character.

The wise 19th century preacher/essayist Henry Ward Beecher (it was his sister, Harriet Beecher Stowe who penned *Uncle Tom's Cabin*) had this to say about character: **"It is not what a man gets but what a man is that he should think of. He should think first of his character, and then of his condition, for if he have the former, he need have no fear about the latter. Character will draw condition after it. Circumstances obey principles."**

Beecher packs a lot of wallop into that paragraph. Given that we live in a world where success is often pegged to material accretion, it is beneficial to step back a pace or two for perspective. He suggests that who you are is ultimately more to be valued that what you are (status, position, vocation). He would agree, I am sure, that a janitor with values is to be prized over a CEO without. He would be right to do so.

A good part of a person's character lies in their ability

to jump into a project with both feet. An old Latin proverb says, *Initium est dimidium facti* **(Once you've started, you're halfway there)**. [*Curtis: What does that mean?* Fair question. It means that it's the beginning that is the hardest part of any venture. Once you get past that huge barrier, the actual doing almost comes off as the easier part.] Nothing of value ever got done by timid people.

President Harry S Truman didn't mince words about this notion: "**Make no little plans. Make the biggest one you can think of, and spend the rest of your life carrying it out**." He's talking about passion, of course, and a life lived without passion ends up an empty shell, hollow and echoing in its barren vacuity.

It is easy, in light of that, to fall into the trap of believing yourselves unworthy of a great challenge. Admiral William F. "Bull" Halsey had an excellent rejoinder to that feeling when he said, "**There are no great men, only great challenges that ordinary men are forced by circumstances to meet**." Indeed, when you find your passions in life, each of you will discover correspondingly new resources within yourselves with which to address and fulfill those wondrous and defining passions.

There will be people who will, as you are in the process of defining yourselves, try and push you into one camp or the other, liberal or conservative. I hope that you will resist such efforts to narrow your selves and hamstring your horizons, because there are values on each side that are worth developing, not the least of which is the conservative bent toward preservation and the liberal leaning toward compassion and caring. In so doing, please keep your sense of humor open and alive for such genial hits as Ambrose Bierce's piercing definition (from *The Devil's Dictionary*): **"A Conservative is one who is enamored of existing evils, as distinguished from the Liberal, who wishes to replace them with others."**

My own little contribution to the litany of character takes the following form. Goal number one is, **Happiness**. Rule number one is, **Everything has a price**. Question number one is, **Are you willing to pay**? While most folks are smart enough to desire happiness, far too great a number fail either to recognize the effort that is required to reach that state, or to be ready to put in the hours needed to achieve it. I desperately hope that you two, each in your own way, will find something that rouses your passions to such a pitch that you'll be willing to commit to that passion with every ounce of your heart and soul and, most importantly, effort.

You've probably heard me say this more times than you care, but it is a fair example of what we're talking about here. In my first year as a free lance writer I made barely $3000. But I had made a promise to myself. I vowed to give myself a full five years to get to the point of making a living at my craft, and if I couldn't reach that point in five years . . . I'd give myself another five years! The point, of course, is that I was willing to undergo any trial, weather any insult, exert any effort necessary to achieve a goal that would grant me happiness beyond all my dreams.

As I watch you two grow—Tamara with your horizon-less

creativity, Curtis with your doggedly logical mind—I wonder what will spark your passionate juices. Hard as it is to stand back, your mother and I will continue to do our best to prepare you for whatever it is that sparks *your* imaginations, putting aside what we might think would be best for you. You do get to live your own lives, in the end, no matter what it seems like for all the moments you've yet known, short of your maturity. In reality, I can't wait to see your eyes light up when the realization smacks you in the middle of the forehead, when you *know* what it is that you're meant to do in this life. It's a wonderfully thrilling moment, and I desperately hope that you'll be willing to pay that price, whatever it is, to fashion out of your dreams a most satisfying reality.

In defining your character, I fervently hope that you will not fall prey to the "modern" trap of specialization. That's why I push reading, in all fields, so strongly. No matter how much you love your chosen profession, it will be expanded and enhanced markedly by every bit of outside information and experience you bring to play upon it. That's why I love Robert Heinlein's following exhortation from his *The Notebooks of Lazarus Long*: "**A human being should be able to change a diaper, plan an invasion, butcher a hog, conn a ship, design a building, write a sonnet, balance accounts, build a wall, set a bone, comfort the dying, take orders, give orders, cooperate, act alone, pitch manure, solve equations, analyze a new problem, program a computer, cook a tasty meal, fight efficiently, die gallantly. Specialization is for insects.**"

How we deal with adversity delineates a good portion of our character. While Admiral James Stockdale was in a Viet Cong Prisoner of War camp for seven years, he came up with what we now call the "Stockdale Paradox" as a means of retaining his sanity and bolstering his resistance. He was able to maintain and benefit from the dynamic tension between the opposites: 1) **Life couldn't possibly be worse than it is at this moment**, and 2) **Someday, things will be better than they ever have been**. The strength those thoughts gave him helped him to survive the trial, and emerge a man stronger for the experience.

Part of the strength may have come from the unconscious notion that is so artfully expressed by Gabriel Marcel, who wrote, **"Hope is a memory of the future."** That, too, seems something of a conundrum, doesn't it? How can we have a "memory" of something that has not yet come to pass in our lives? Perhaps it has something to do with a cultural memory that we're all born with, and only need to tap in times dire and stressful. Perhaps.

It helps, I think, to avoid the trap of thinking that some people are "lucky," while others are not. There is a wonderful Chinese parable that I am going to shorten here for your benefit. A nobleman's prized stallion runs off one day. His neighbors bemoan his bad luck. He says, **"What is luck?"** A few days later, the stallion returns leading a herd of wild horses. The lord's neighbors chorus, "What good luck!" He says, **"What is luck?"** His son, training and breaking the wild horses, breaks his arm. The chorus? "What bad luck!"

The lord? **"What is luck?"** War breaks out, but the lord's son is exempted from serving by his injury. Chorus: "What good luck!" Response: **"What is luck?"** The moral? Life deals you a deck of cards. Play them without complaint. Better still, play them with enthusiasm, with passion, with heart.

Perhaps a better slant was taken by the Prussian diplomat Baron Wilhelm von Humboldt, who advised, **"How a person masters his fate is more important than what his fate is."** You are who you are, no matter what happens around you. How you respond to the challenges of your lives will determine the extent and depth of your character. I hope both of you develop the sort of character that will sustain your selves and your personalities through whatever trials life tosses at you. [*Curtis: I do believe I can do all the things that come at me in life. Most of the time.*]

LET YOUR SPIRITS RISE

Being half German, I like things to be at least a little organized. Thus, I have come to what I call my "theory of selves," which suggests that we each have four "selves," each of which needs to be nurtured, fed, exercised and put to good use lest we not be operating at full power. Those selves are the spiritual, the mental, the physical and the social.

As strongly as I believe in the preeminence of the spiritual self, I am not wont to count out the value of religion as a motivating force. Where religion stays close to morals-driven values, it has much to offer. But I am quite wary of those organized entities that differ from cults only in the degree in which they strip their subjects of self, individuality, identity. Any religion that puts property before ethics and values strikes me as utterly devoid of spirituality.

The vaunted Zen master, D. T. Suziki's take on Christianity was insightful and incisive, wry and biting: **"God against man. Man against man. Man against woman. Man against nature. Very strange religion."** If you think about it, there is a lot of tension built into Christianity, and rather less the sense of oneness that comes out of Zen, or its progenitor, Buddhism.

I am very much inclined to agree with the Dalai Lama Bstan-'Dzin-Rgya-Mtscho, who wrote in 1999, **"Spirituality I take to be concerned with those qualities of the human spirit—such as love and compassion, patience, tolerance, forgiveness, contentment, a sense of responsibility, a sense of harmony—which bring happiness to both self and others. . . . This is why I** sometimes say that religion is something we can perhaps do without. What we cannot do without are these basic spiritual qualities."

"**Religion without joy is no religion.**" Theodore Parker. That's another clue. I distrust any religion that is so serious, so contra to the essential juices of life as to throw a wet blanket over emotion and feeling. Better, I think, is the almost whimsical admonition of Rabbi Shemaiah, who lived a half century before Christ: "**Love work, hate tyranny, live righteously . . . and don't let your name become too well known to the authorities!**"

How you approach the spiritual quest that ought to inform your life has a lot to do with what you'll get out of that journey, kids. I think that the English philosopher Francis Bacon had the right approach when he posited, "**If we begin with certainties, we shall end in doubts; but, if we begin with doubts, and are patient in them, we shall end in certainties.**" That makes a lot more sense to me. What do you think?

The novelist Barbara Kingsolver—you must read her delightful books *The Bean Trees* and *Pigs in Heaven*— puts faith under the light of reason. Says she, "**Faith, by definition, is impervious to fact. A belief that can be changed by new information was probably a scientific one, not a religious one, and science derives its value from its openness to revision.**" Or, as I have reminded friends, "**You can't argue someone out of a position they were never argued into in the first place.**" Logic works from one side of the brain, emotion works from the other. Still, the emotional component is not to be put aside. The soul is essential to the equation, and none puts it better than John Nance. Says he, "**The soul may be the part of you that sees the dream.**" There have to be dreams. Without them, life is cruelly circumscribed, woefully diminished. [*Curtis: I think if people have faith in themselves they can do many things in life.*]

Given that process of analysis, it strikes me that the dynamic tension of opposites usually best gets us to some point of overall understanding. As the wonderful Yiddish writer Isaac Bashevis Singer once wrote, **"We must believe in free will. We have no choice."**

Any duality demonstrates the same lesson. Life and death. Chaos and creation. Entropy and life. Being and nothingness. The thought of being either a single grain of sand on an endless beach or the very center of the universe. In each case, the one or the other, standing alone, is something of a caricature: silly, unbalanced, and of not much use. But the dynamic tension of the polar ideas, when crossed, when examined, when tested by thought and by experience gives us a balance at the center, an insight into the greater meaning of it all. Assesses the Israeli scholar Adin Steinsaltz, **"I see sanity as the ability to be both extremes at one time, jolly and sad, a balance between Heaven and Hell."**

That means that some sense of activism, some sense of participation is essential to a spiritual life well lived. Reminded the 18th century philosopher Edmund Burke,

"The only thing necessary for the triumph of evil is for good men to do nothing."

A big part of becoming sound, spiritually, has to do with one of the lessons I learned in law school, that of looking to substance over form. There is, I think, almost an inherent modesty to favoring the substance of the spiritual to the form, materialism and ostentation of religion. Such a life would, artlessly, encompass the music of the spheres.

Goethe addressed the same subject of substance versus form far more acerbically when he argued, **"The deed is everything, the fame is nothing."** It is far more important to easily know who you are in your own heart when you retire each evening than to seek any fame or notoriety. The latter can be taken away from you. Not so, the former. As Charles Darwin posited, **"The things that are not seen are eternal!"** Also, it might be easier to be content with that inner, unseen satisfaction if we remember Martin Luther King Jr.'s observation that, **"The arc of the universe is long, but it bends toward justice."**

In similar vein, Albert Einstein: "**Mankind's greatest problem is the perfection of means and the confusion of ends.**" [*Curtis: What does this mean?* It means that we have learned more about creating weapons of total destruction than we have about the morality of creating, and worse, using such weapons.] There are always those Machiavellian souls who will suggest that the ends justify the means, but no good goal can ever be supported by means that are less than ethical, less than moral. If you take the low ground, you will remain tarnished by its dirt, its muck, its mire.

The thing we seek, above all in our quest for a sound spiritual sense, is truth, an understanding well-grounded, universal and incontrovertible. The New England poet/ diplomat James Russell Lowell said it this way:

Get but the truth once uttered, and 'tis like

A star new-born that drops into its place

And which, once circling in its placid round,

Not all the tumult of the earth can shake.

Working toward such truths is a lifetime venture that

requires a certain faith in oneself and a courage capable of overcoming inevitable setbacks. An old mountain man's prayer says, **"Lord, I don't ask for a faith that would move yonder mountain. I can take enough dynamite and move it, if it needs movin'. I pray, Lord, for enough faith to move me."** As to the courage to put that faith to good use, Dr. John Watson wrote, **"Moral courage is obeying one's conscience and doing what one believes to be right, in face of a hostile majority; and moral cowardice is stifling one's conscience, and doing what is less than right to win other people's favor."**

Perhaps the greatest spiritual virtue is that of forgiveness. As the great South African leader, Bishop Desmond Tutu reminds us, forgiveness is a gift that we give to ourselves, a gift that restores human dignity. Wrote Tutu, **"It gives people resilience, enabling them to survive and emerge still human despite all efforts to dehumanize them."** If the Dalai Lama comes at it from a slightly different perspective, the result is nearly the same: **"[When we] shift the focus**

of attention away from self and toward others . . . we

find that the scale of our own problems diminishes."

Similarly, the Jewish religion employs the word *teshuvah*

for the concept of repentance, but the word is a bit more

encompassing, including the deeper understanding of a

look at the entire arc of one's life, a return to grace. Well

worth considering, to my way of thinking.

Does life have meaning? Not inherently, I think. It's not

a given. Rather, I believe that it is our obligation to create a

meaning—with our actions, with our lives—that informs

all of life with every ounce of meaning it will ever need.

A big responsibility? Yes, it is. But it is a responsibility

that will give you a reason to live large. I will not quote

the whole of the poem "Invictus," but invite you to have

a copy and keep it close so that you understand in full

what William Ernst Henley means by his admonition to be

"master of my fate:/ I am the captain of my soul." For it

is only by taking full responsibility for your own personal

spiritual selves that you will be able to infuse your lives

with the meaning they so richly deserve. [*Tamara: I think every individual has their own personal meaning to life. I believe everyone has their own opinion of life's meaning.*]

I leave you, here, with Dante Alighiere's insightful musing: "**. . . light for good and for evil is given to you, and free will, which, though it endures fatigue in the first battles with the heavens, afterwards, if it be well nurtured, overcomes everything.**"

A MIND AT LARGE
IS A GOOD THING

I once wrote a weekly newspaper column called "A Mind at Large." It was something of a "philosophy of life" column. The editors let me assess any subject I wished, and rarely changed a word I wrote. I did that column for nine years. It was the most fun, least paid work I've ever done. I miss it to this day.

The point I am aiming at here is this: Playing with your mind, making it work, pushing it to remain open, pliable and nimble is an ongoing and constant challenge. Indeed, the medicos have recently discovered that older folks who consciously exercise their minds—by reading, by playing chess, by discussing issues with friends and kin—cut their risk of Alzheimer's by more than half. In the medical field, any trial that is effective by "more than half" is a rousing, big time, shout-it-to-the-newspapers success.

My clear and all-time favorite in this arena goes to Supreme Court Justice Oliver Wendell Holmes Jr., who observed that "**A mind expanded by a new idea never returns to its former size**." The whole point of learning, in a nutshell, is to expand one's horizons and open one's experiences, to put zest and flavor into one's life.

That's why you should challenge, harass and fight those who would narrow our mental landscapes with every fiber of your being. "**Wherever they burn books,**" wrote Heinrich Heine, "**they will also, in the end, burn human beings.**" Thus, your education is a most precious commodity, one that you should value and protect. As Malcolm Forbes liked to remind his business associates,

"Education's purpose is to replace an empty mind with an open one." Or, to turn that to its obverse side, the clever bumper sticker: **"If you think education is expensive, try ignorance."** There is nothing ever in this world that will get you into trouble quicker and deeper than the absence of knowledge.

It's not that you have to be a genius to succeed. Only that you constantly push back at the frontiers of your knowledge. Besides, as Arthur Koestler pointed out, **"The principal mark of genius is not perfection but originality, the opening of new frontiers."** If you read, if you expose yourself to ideas, old as well as new, you set the foundation for original thinking.

President Harry S Truman was a reader of history, and understood its value as a discipline. Said the one-time haberdasher, **"The only thing new in the world is the history you haven't read."** 'Tis true. [*Curtis: I think it's cool that you don't have to stop learning in life, that there's always something else to learn.*] The world seems to operate on a cyclical nature. We like to say, What goes around comes around. The *Bible* says it, "**As ye sow, so shall ye reap**." The computer gang's original take is "**garbage in, garbage out**." In other words, we know how people respond to certain stimuli. If we keep on beating our heads against the wall, it's going to cause some damage. Or, as Sancho Panza (*Don Quixote*) reminds us, "**Whether the stone hits the pitcher, or the pitcher hits the stone . . . it's going to be *bad* for the pitcher**." Got it?

I've always pushed you two to read a lot. Sometimes you really enjoy it, sometimes you rail against. Even when you're feeling "anti," we read nonetheless. Because, a book can take you anywhere in place, anywhere in time, anywhere in all the many ethers. If you can imagine it, it's likely that someone else has been there, too, and written something about it that will expand your mind with a new idea, a new notion about how the world can be looked at.

The marvelous historian, Barbara W. Tuchman, said it better than I can: "**Books are the carriers of civilization.**

Without books, history is silent, literature dumb, science crippled, thought and speculation at a standstill." In short, nothing works at or near its potential without the mind-expanding experience that others offer though the written word.

You learn almost as much from writing. "**Reading maketh a full man, conference a ready man, and writing an exact man**," counseled Francis Bacon. The reading, in and of itself, is merely the intake of information. But that information is put to far better use if it is challenged in discussion, then put to the final test by the arrangements of your own thoughts in transferring them to paper. That's always been the power of the press, the power of the written word: Readers assume that the writer has thought things through to the point of at least near certainty, if not to certainty itself.

As for the art and craft of writing itself? It stretches you like no other discipline does, for it requires you to investigate the far corners of your experiences and beliefs. The effort that is required? The very mold for sportswriters,

Red Smith, put it this way: **"Writing is easy. I just open a vein and bleed."**

I have great admiration for poets, who are somehow capable of distilling a thought down to its brandy-essence. I have attempted poems—more to bring better cadence and improved sound to my prose—but have yet to write a single one that is memorable to myself. Robert Frost, on the other hand, penned hundreds. When asked to describe the process, his explanation was, **"You start with an idea. Then you ride it like a horse until it's a poem."** [*Curtis: Poetry is fun because you can write a poem about anything!*] Carl Sandburg distilled it still further: **"Poetry is an echo, asking a shadow to dance."** Ah ha!

The wonder of our minds lies in their breadth. We can journey to galaxies beyond the most powerful telescopes we have yet built and, at almost the selfsame instant, we can probe the very depths of our innermost souls. The philosopher Immanuel Kant, at the conclusion of his *Critique of Practical Reason*, writes, **"Two things fill the**

mind with ever-increasing wonder and awe, the more often and the more intensely the mind of thought is drawn to them: the starry heavens above me and the moral law within me."

That moral law is so important. Without it, you are like a tiller-less boat in an angry sea. William Hazlitt wrote, **"Man is the only animal that laughs and weeps; for he is the only animal that is struck with the difference between what things are, and what they ought to be."** (Mark Twain was a bit more cynical: **"Man is the only animal that blushes . . . or needs to!"**) Because we have a brain, and with it the power to comprehend death long before its onset, we correspondingly have the responsibility to exercise the power of thought beneficially and with compassion. George Bernard Shaw said it so poetically that Robert F. Kennedy borrowed it often: **"You see things: and you say 'Why?' But I dream things that never were; and I say 'Why not?'"**

The starry heavens intrigue as well. I hope both of you

will always keep your minds open to what new insights dwell in the incredible vastness of space. More than two millennia ago the Greek philosopher Metrodorus proffered, **"To consider the Earth as the only world with life in all of space is as absurd as to believe that in an entire field sown with grain only one plant will grow."**

It is helpful to keep a sense of balance when working the mind. To stick too closely to one discipline is to rob yourself of the cross-pollinating advantages of others, just as cross-training in athletics brings freshness and new perspectives to the sport you love most. It's important to take time off, too, to just loaf, to rest, to recharge the batteries. As you know, I usually work only three or four hours each morning, giving my afternoons over to you guys, reading, and some athletic endeavor, the better, the more animatedly to face the next work day. Leonardo da Vinci, perhaps the wisest man ever to walk this earth, put it this way: **"Every now and then, go away, take a little relaxation, because when you come back to your work,**

your judgment will be surer. To remain constantly at work will cause you to lose power of judgment. Go some distance away, because then the work appears smaller and more of it can be taken in at a glance, and a lack of harmony or proportion is more readily seen."

Curtis, you have a Teutonic mind, one that perceives order, appreciates it, finds it, creates it. Everything in your room seems to have its own proper place. You do well in math, and seem to enjoy its challenges, so that may be your highest arena, creatively. Just remember never to censor yourself when you are pursuing something new, something different. As Malcolm Hein said it, **"There is little room left for wisdom when one is full of judgment."**

Tamara, your mind works in a different fashion, finding patterns far outside of the norm. I always think of you when I think of George Carlin's line, **"Those who dance are considered insane by those who don't hear the music."** Creativity, you will find, is a difficult challenge, and there will be those who would damper your talents. Don't let them. They probably don't hear your music.

Wordsworth spoke of Sir Isaac Newton—the man who turned a falling apple into the Theory of Gravity—"**the index of his mind, voyaging strange seas of thought, alone**." The creative mind necessarily travels uncharted paths. That is its definition. Don't be afraid to go there. The rest of us will follow, given enough time and exposure. Don't forget, many thought of Einstein as vague and Mozart as addle-brained. They were wrong both times.

The way we see things has a lot to do with creativity. Michelangelo, as sculptor, said that he could look at a block of marble and see the work of art inside it, and that his only responsibility was to "**remove that which was not the sculpture**." Which is easy if you can see what he sees. Few of us have that sort of vision. You do, Miss Tama.

So always keep your eyes and minds open to the new experience. Creativity cannot exist in a world without endless and open horizons. As the curmudgeonly Canadian novelist Robertson Davies once wrote, **"A Philistine is someone who is content to live in a wholly unexplored world."** Please be wildly unafraid to explore the worlds you experience.

RESPECT YOUR
BODY, TOO

One of the things you'll discover before too long is that your body will renege on you if you don't give it the same feeding, the same nurturing, the same exercise that you provide your other "selves." I know you've chuckled as you've watched me struggle through my new-found enthusiasm for yoga these last few months ("breathe normally while you hold the position"), but its practice has given me a new insight into taking care of the physical self. Just the breathing exercises themselves—entirely apart from the obvious benefits the stretching has given me in playing baseball and tennis (in terms of flexibility, endurance and freedom from injury)—have helped me to better put into practice the concept of slowing my life down to a point where time nearly ceases to have meaning. The discipline has helped me to put time, as a consideration, at a far lower point on the totem pole of consequence, so much so that it has, at the same time, taken a good deal of tension out of my life. As you grow older, you will easily recognize the value of taking most of a day's ordinary tensions out of play.

One of the things you will learn about your bodies is that they do not take care of themselves, wondrously constructed as they are. It is vital to learn that you are responsible for your body's care and feeding, for making sure that it is tuned and fit for what you will ask of it. If you fail in that responsibility, no one else can or will do it for you, in this venue or in others. Even Shakespeare, in *Julius Caesar*, wasn't above reminding us that how we take care of ourselves is up to us, and not the fates. "**Men at some time**

are masters of their fates: The fault, dear Brutus, is not in our stars, But in ourselves, that we are underlings." To make something of our bodies, of ourselves, it is up to us.

As you have learned growing up, I place a high value on participating in sports as a means of staying in shape and having fun at the same time. You also know how important fair play and sportsmanship are to me. I've tried hard to inculcate in you the Zen notion of putting the goal—winning, results—to the side in favor of focusing on the act, the participation itself. The irony of putting winning on the back burner is that you have a greater chance at good results if you are so loose that winning and losing are irrelevant. The late A's and Yankee pitcher, Jim "Catfish" Hunter, voiced the notion rather well when he said, **"Winning isn't everything; trying to win is."** [*Tamara: I totally agree. I think it's worth it to give it your all and not care if you win or lose. But if you're just in it to win, then you shouldn't be playing. I don't think it's a life or death situation.* You'd appreciate the late Bobby Riggs' statement that, "Tennis isn't a matter of life and death—it's much more important!"]

It is the effort, the practice, the process that is truly important. I know you've heard this from me before, but it is vital enough to repeat: **"It's all practice."** [*Curtis: I need to learn this one better, that I shouldn't worry so much about winning.*] Or this other, to emphasize the value of repetition in perfecting a skill, be it an arpeggio on the piano or turning the double play: **"It's nothing that another ten thousand repetitions won't cure."** Yes, that does seem daunting at the outset, but if you focus on the process, on the practice, it gets easier, and easier, and easier. Almost before you realize it, skill sneaks up on you, envelops you, captures you. It is a wonderful and empowering feeling, this working up to a competency. Once you achieve it in one area of your life, it becomes geometrically easier to apply it to other aspects.

One part of the physical self that is rarely addressed concerns making do with less, in terms of material things.

Henry David Thoreau, in *Walden*, says that "**A man is wealthy in proportion to that which he can afford to leave alone**."

It is an attitude, I think, which says that "who I am" is far more valuable than what I acquire. William Henry Channing says it a little better: "**To live content with small means; to seek elegance rather than luxury, and refinement rather than fashion; to be worthy, not respectable, and wealthy, not rich; to study hard, think quietly, talk gently, act frankly; to listen to stars and birds, to babes and sages, with open heart; to bear all cheerfully, do all bravely, await occasions, hurry never. In a word, to let the spiritual, unbidden and unconscious, grow up through the common. This is my symphony**." This quote, above all, shows you how interconnected all our selves and all our disciplines necessarily are.

Part of the problem comes with our expecting life to be easy and in the absence of physical effort. Economist John Kenneth Galbraith pointed to that in *The Affluent*

Society, saying, "**What is called a high standard of living consists, in considerable measure, in arrangements for avoiding muscular energy, for increasing sensual pleasure and enhancing caloric intake above any conceivable nutritional requirement**." The discipline of caring properly for your body includes not only a useful exercise regimen, but also a diet that provides sufficient energy without overdosing. An overdose on food is just as damaging, in the long run, as an overdose on drugs. That's why I try to keep to my "Rule of One," which dictates that, when I have to have a candy bar . . . I have only one (of the miniatures). Okay, sometimes I sneak an extra, but most of the time I stick to my rule. The same with food: one portion at a sitting. It's plenty. We Americans are more than blessed with access to food, and more often than not eat more than a bit more than is necessary for optimal health. A little discipline at the table can go a long way to improving your physical health.

Try not to get down on yourself when you fail to reach

your goals. Sliding from one candy bar to two, eating that extra helping, those things happen. Just remember that they don't have to be permanent. The first or second time I went back to Atlanta to meet your mother's parents, I feasted on Cafa's bacon-laden breakfasts . . . and shot up to 205 pounds! Aieee! My body instantly told me that that was twenty pounds more than my frame could easily carry. It took a few months to whittle them off, but whittle them off I did.

You have known your mother and me to be almost daily consumers of wine with dinner, but you have never seen either of us in any way incapacitated by over-consumption. A glass or two with dinner, and that's about it. Wine, like aspirin, is a drug, and there is a beneficial dosage and a toxic dosage, and it is essential that you know the difference. I've always liked Charles Dickens' assessment (in *Oliver Twist*) of a man who did not: **"If he were really not in the habit of drinking rather more than was exactly good for him, he might have brought an action against his countenance**

for libel, and have recovered heavy damages." Ha! Don't you love it!

I'm not quite sure where to work this in, so it might as well be now. Sensuality and sexuality are wonderful things. Especially at your age, folks will attempt to convince you that sensuality is the devil incarnate and sex is worse. They are wrong in the blanket approach; they are right only in the time-sensitive category. At your age, you need to be wary of both, but not unaware. As you mature, I hope that you both will find pleasure in respectful touching, both the sensual touching of massage, a worthy hug, a clap on the back and the sexual touching that becomes appropriate and necessary when you find the mature love that sets off the fireworks, the silly grins and, best, the laughter of love that eases the belly and fires the brain. You'll know, in every fiber of your being when the time is right. You'll also know, if you listen to your body, and know its responses, when it's wrong. Just remember to listen. Just as your body tells you when you are sated with food, it will tell you when the time is "not now" for sensuality and sexuality. Just remember to listen.

One of my favorite quotes is from an 85-year-old Kentucky woman, who talks about going "barefoot earlier in the spring." As I grow older, I agree with this simple, most wonderful physical expression of our bodies touching the earth in a way that farmers once did without even thinking about it. Said Nadine Stair, **"If I had my life to live over, I'd dare to make more mistakes next time. I would be sillier than I have been this time. I would take fewer things seriously. I would take more chances. I would take more trips. I would climb more mountains and swim more rivers. I would eat more ice cream and less beans. I would perhaps have more actual troubles, but I'd have fewer imaginary ones. . . . Oh, I've had my moments, and if I had it to do over again, I'd have more of them. In fact, I'd try to have nothing else. Just moments, one after another, instead of living so many years ahead of each day.**

"**I've been one of those persons who never goes anywhere without a thermometer, a hot water bottle, a raincoat, and a parachute. If I had it to do over again, I would travel lighter than I have. . . . I would start barefoot earlier in the spring and stay that way later in the fall. I would go to more dances. I would ride more merry-go-rounds. I would pick more daisies.**" Listen to your body. It will tell you what it needs if you are so attuned. And, as the local disk jockey once advised, "**Don't walk; dance!**"

I'M A SOCIABLE FELLOW

We might consider the social "self" not as essential as, say, the physical self. We might be wrong to do so. Just look at the studies which indicate that infants who are not touched, who are not held, who are not cuddled . . . will "fail to thrive." Die. That's right, die. Turns out we are very much social animals. Perhaps not so needy as sheep, but maybe the gap isn't all that great, either.

As you begin building and shaping your social selves, I hope that humility will be one of your building blocks. It's a good one to start with. As the 17th century French moralist Jean de La Bruyere wrote, "**Modesty is to merit** what shade is to figures in a picture, it gives it strength and makes it stand out."

Humility, to be effective, needs to be balanced with courage and strength, too. In the middle of all that, it's good to keep a solid sense of humor close at hand, tied closely to a sense of impishness. Heed, then, the words of Lin Yutang (*The Importance of Living*): "**In this present age of threats to democracy and individual liberty, probably only the scamp and the spirit of the scamp alone will save us from becoming lost as serially numbered units in the masses of disciplined, obedient, regimented and uniformed coolies. The scamp will be the last and most formidable enemy of dictatorships. He will be the champion of human dignity and individual freedom, and will be the last to be conquered. All modern civilization depends entirely upon him.**" Tom Sawyer? Scamp. Henry David Thoreau? Lenny Bruce? Ambrose Bierce? Scamps, all. Definitely something to aspire to.

In the end, happiness is pretty much a choice we make

for ourselves, and I hope that you both will opt to live happy lives. You seem predisposed to do so at this point. In *Animal Dreams* Barbara Kingsolver says it thusly: "**I've about decided that's the main thing that separates happy people from the other people: the feeling that you're a practical item, with a use, like a sweater or a socket wrench.**" Which means, I think, that you become a person who contributes something positive to the mix of society, and not merely draw down on the principle of human knowledge and experience that's accrued over the millennia.

I suppose it is my innate sensitivity (which you especially share, Curtis), but I have little or no patience with those who would deny any rights of sociability with those different in race, religion or viewpoint. "**Brotherhood is not so wild a dream as those who profit by postponing it pretend,**" said Edwin Corwin. Under the skin, we are all the same. Period.

And when you stand up for the rights of those with less

currency than yourselves, be bolstered by the ringing words of social philosopher John Stuart Mill, who wrote in *On Liberty*, **"If all mankind minus one were of one opinion, mankind would be no more justified in silencing that one person than he, if he had the power, would be justified in silencing mankind. . . . We can never be sure that the opinion we are endeavoring to stifle is a false opinion; and if we were sure, stifling it would be an evil still."** Stand up for your beliefs, always and against all odds. [*Tamara: I strongly agree. I think that if someone believes in something enough to stand up for it, they should. Even if others don't feel the same. I say stand up for what you believe is right, even if you're the only one standing.*]

Remember, it wasn't all that long ago, in the greater scheme of things, when the practice of slavery was accepted in this enlightened country (and still is, in backward areas of the third planet, even in our new millennium). Fortunately, there were those, lead by gentle Quakers and others who saw a more graceful world, who initiated the seed of change by challenging the *status quo*. As Oscar Wilde reminded, **"Discontent is the first step in the progress of a man or a nation."** Discontent, along with standing up to be counted, to have your say no matter how many stand against you.

For me, that discontent is capital punishment. If it does not deter, as I believe, if it serves only savagery in terms of retribution, as I believe, then it must be ended. Okay, I'll step down from the soap box. But everyone should have some cause, some wrong that requires righting. There are enough to go around, believe me. The thing is, when you do contribute something bettering, something beneficial to our society, it has a moral grandeur that can be quite spectacular and quietly satisfying.

The most mysterious aspect of life is its end, for we do not know whether death is mere transition or if we find ultimate humility as fertilizer. William Saroyan, in *The Human Comedy* posited that, **"The person of a man may leave—or be taken away—but the best part of a good man stays. It stays forever. Love is immortal and makes**

all things immortal. But hate dies every minute." A rather graceful thought, don't you think?

To extend that thought, be wary of the allure of anger because it always seems to bite its possessor. As the Buddha counseled, **"Holding on to anger is like grasping a hot coal with the intent of throwing it at someone else—you are the one who gets burned."**

One part of anger management concerns the politics of war. Your Grandpa George served as a pharmacist's mate in the Navy in World War II. Two of my uncles served time in prison rather than betray their religious principles against war. I was ironically spared the agony of decision during Viet Nam by a high lottery number. In many conversations with my good friend, your "Uncle" Tim, we both agree that we do not want our children to have to go to war, no matter how "just" the cause may appear. We are guided, in part, by English psychologist Alan McGlashan's brief bromide—**"To the eyes of Reason war is the total eclipse of meaning"**—and by his countryman Wilfred Owen's mind-expanding anti-war poem *"Dulce Et Decorum Est"* decrying the patriotic lie that **"It is sweet and good to die for one's country."** Tragically, Owen died a very young man in the gaseous trenches of World War I.

If you prefer, please refer to the Mathew Broderick film "War Games," in which the computer Joshua sums it all up thusly: **"A strange game. The only winning move is not to play."** When it comes to war, that is the only winning move: Don't take delivery. Don't play. Because it isn't play at all. It is merely destruction. As one pundit says, **"You can no more win a war than you can win an earthquake."**

There will come a time in your life when you will be put in a position of authority over others. Aside from the Golden Rule—**Do unto others as you would have them do unto you**—Dag Hammarskjold, the late Attorney General of the United Nations, wisely advised, **"Your position never gives you the right to command. It only imposes on you the duty of so living your life that others can receive your orders without being humiliated."** Set a good example by your own lives, and those who look up to you will have someone worth looking up to, worth emulating. [*Curtis: I always try to do to my friends what I would want them to do to me.* You do. What I like even more is that you, and Tamara, are equally gentle and kind to those younger and less powerful than you are.]

Rabbi Hillel the Elder, commenting on the ultimate meaning of Judaism, said it this way: "**What is hateful to thee, do not unto thy fellowman; this is the whole law; the rest is mere commentary.**" It's that sensitivity we were talking about earlier. If you feel it, surely others will as well.

Do not lose sight of the community you live in, and the responsibility you have to help those less blessed than yourselves. And do not ever think that you are not blessed: You have two parents who love you plenty, you are fed and clothed as you are loved, to excess, and you have equal educational opportunities (to excess). Counseled the Quaker missionary and prison reformer Etienne de Grelett, "**I pass**

through this world but once. If, therefore there is a good that I can do, let me do it now: let me not deter nor neglect it, for I shall not pass this way again." Similarly, with grit, from Black Panther leader Eldrige Cleaver, "**If you're not a part of the solution, you're a part of the problem.**" In the end, we are not merely our brother's keeper, we *are* our brother. There is no way to keep one's respect if others are wanting.

At the heart of our social self is the grandest relationship of all, love. I hope that your mother and I have set a good example for you in that department, by respecting each other with great and enduring fondness. People often quote Christ (in St. Matthew), but leave out the last two words. They are important. "**Thou shalt love thy neighbor *as thyself***" (italics mine). The crux of love is that you cannot offer it from an empty vessel. Unless you have esteem and love for yourself you have nothing to give to your partner, and love is *entirely* about giving.

It is all too easy in the fast-paced life we are bidden (by

advertisers) to lead to mix our emotions. Revel Howe sorted it out nicely when he observed that, **"We too often love things and use people, when we should be using things and loving people."** Keep those two sorted out, and you will be well ahead of the game.

The poet Rainer Maria Rilke looked at love and suggested, **"Love consists in this, that two solitudes protect and touch and greet each other."** Or, from another angle (this from French aviator/philosopher Antoine de Saint-Exupery): **"Love does not consist in gazing at each other, but in looking outward together in the same direction."** Love is not a giving up of yourself, but rather a vast and unexplainable expansion of yourself, into and around another. It is the absolute best of what life has to offer, amid all its glories.

But always remember, too, as my friend Ken Coburn likes to say, **"Love isn't glue."** It isn't meant to stifle. As in any relationship, there will be disagreements. The trick is to work through them to the goal, not of winning, but of learning. As A. P. Herbert observed, "**The concept of two people living together for 25 years without a serious dispute suggests a lack of spirit only to be admired in sheep.**" Better still, I return you to Rilke: "**A good marriage is that in which each appoints the other guardian of his solitude. Once the realization is accepted that even between the closest human beings infinite distances continue to exist, a wonderful living side by side can grow up, if they succeed in loving the distance between them which makes it possible for each to see the other whole and against a wide sky.**"

It's like I always tell your mother: As one of us grows, we bring the other up the ladder of growth with us; as the other grows, he or she brings the other up as well in a constant and on-going leapfrog dance of learning and actualization. We feed off one another, we egg each other on, we are cheerleaders, each for the other. It is a wondrous feeling, believe me.

When you find that one great relationship, and (if you

so choose) have children of your own, remember that kids haven't really changed all that much over the years. Listen to this timeless tirade against the habits of youngsters: **"Our youth now love luxury. They have bad manners, contempt for authority; they show disrespect for their elders, and love chatter in place of exercise. They no longer rise when others enter the room. They contradict their parents, chatter before company, gobble their food, and tyrannize their teachers."** Sounds so modern, doesn't it? Makes me laugh out loud to remind myself that those lines were written more than two thousand years ago . . . by Socrates. (Cue the laughter. Ha!)

If you become parents, I hope that you will be sensitive to the needs and especially *feelings* of your children (my grandchildren). Keep in mind the diaries of Charles Francis Adams (the son of John Quincy Adams) and his son Brooke Adams. One day they went fishing together. The father's diary entry was this: "Went fishing with my son. A day wasted." Brooke's diary entry for the same day? **"Went**

fishing with my father—the most glorious day of my life." (Perhaps it's just a question of perspective. There is the old story of two boys whose fathers both work at the same factory. One simply says that his dad is a riveter, but the other exclaims, **"My dad builds airplanes!"**)

Bessie Anderson wraps up the social whirl for me rather artfully. Said she, **"He has achieved success who has lived well, laughed often and loved much: . . . who has left the world better than he found it; . . . who has always looked for the best in others and given them the best he had; whose life was an inspiration; whose memory a benediction."** So please, Curt and Tama, aspire to live lives that will be a guiding beacon, to my grandchildren and to all others whose lives come into your spheres of influence. You may not realize it, but that number will be far larger than you might ever imagine. Do it first for your own sakes; but do it also for theirs.

AND IN CLOSING . . .

Perhaps the greatest of the lessons I have learned in my half century and change is that concerning time and its best use. I am not sure that it can be learned at so tender an age as you are at now—teens are in such a rush and such a bustle to grow up and do and be—but if you can absorb the lesson, you will find it to be of inestimable value. Baba Ram Dass called it *Be Here Now* in his book of the same name. It is the lesson of living each moment in full awareness of that moment, to the complete exclusion of past and future, to the complete exclusion of numbing nostalgia and wasteful wishes that are, in the end, projections of weakness and irresponsibility.

The supporting quote for this understanding might seem weak or insubstantial at quick glance, but stick with it for a bit. It comes from Annie Dillard, in *The Writing Life*. Says she, "**How we spend our days is, of course, how we spend our lives**." The key word is, I believe, *spend*. I say that because the endless succession of "moments" we live, something of an "eternal now," is the very currency of our lives. Thus, it behooves us to invest this capital wisely, and *spend* it with great awareness and understanding of what it is we are giving up each and every one of those moments. If we squander them, they are wasted. But if we patiently put them to good and useful purposes, then we shall live our future moments with exquisite equity and memorable reflections.

Building that equity comes by way of expending our moments fully and with some sense of gusto. I think it was Vera, in *Auntie Mame*, who reminded us that, "**Life is a**

feast . . . but most damned fools are starving to death!" If you are bashful and reticent about claiming your life, it will slide past you in the flick of an eyelash. If, on the other hand, you aggressively grasp onto life as if it were a bucking bull, it spreads out in a panorama of such length and depth as to be positively breathtaking. Time, in effect, seems to stand still, just for you. In short, you get so much more return on your investment by diving into life's grand meal and scarffing up life's substance to its fullest than by sitting on the sidelines and watching the meal be downed by others.

In the final scene of the play *Our Town*, Emily, who has just been buried, looks back over those who remain, the living. She muses, **"Do any human beings ever realize life while they live it?—every, every minute."** Carl Sandburg extends that thought thusly: **"Time is the coin of your life. It is the only coin you have, and only you can determine how it will be spent. Be careful lest you let other people spend it for you."** There's that word again, *spend*. Dillard is right, Sandburg is right. If you let other people and other circumstances dictate how your lives are spent, the sands of time will fall through your hourglasses swiftly and without remorse, and your lives will be gone, spent and squandered in a nanosecond. Better to take control of your time, of your lives, and *choose* how they are to be spent, how they are to be lived.

There is a joke I recall, where a Mexican reminds his *gringo* friend that *mañana* doesn't mean "tomorrow," it just means "not today." The Mexican author, Carlos Fuentes puts it rather more elegantly, more eloquently when he expands that thought to its more meaningful conclusion: **"The Mexican *mañana* does not mean putting things off 'til the morrow. It means not letting the future intrude on the sacred completeness of today."** Do you see the difference? I hope so.

It is also important that we extend our joy in life to others. The wonderful physician/humanist Albert Schwitzer put it this way: "**Until he extends his circle of compassion to all living things, man will not himself find peace.**"

Don't ever be afraid of demanding better of yourself and for yourself. As Joseph Wood Krutch once pointed out, "**Cats seem to go on the principle that it never does any harm to ask for what you want.**" Your Grandpa George came at the same principle edgewise: "**Never ask a question if you can't take 'no' for the answer.**" If you combine those, you come up with a more assertive principle: Go for it! Ernest Hemingway's *Old Man and the Sea* was turned down by more than 100 publishers, but he refused to take each "no" as the final determinant of that book's inestimable and enduring value. That is why I ask you to adhere to philosopher Henri Begson's admonition, "*Je suis une chose qui dure*" ("**I am a thing that lasts**").

In a similar vein, pay heed to playwright/prime minister Vaclav Havel's musing on the subject of hope. "**Hope is not the conviction that something will turn out well but the certainty that something makes sense, regardless of**

how it turns out." When you believe in what you are doing, stick to your guns no matter what any or all say against you. To support yourself, against dire development, fall back on Aristotle, that wise old man who affirmed, "**The secret of happiness is action, the exercise of energy in a way suited to a man's nature and circumstances.**"

Hope comes most easily to those of us who are able to create some sense of meaningfulness to our lives. The Auschwitz survivor Viktor E. Frankl wrote that meaning can be discovered in three ways, "**by creating a work or doing a deed; by experiencing something or encountering someone; and by the attitude we take toward unavoidable suffering.**" The key to that is the understanding that *we* carve out the meaning of our lives for ourselves. It comes from the agency of no other person and no other thing. It comes from within. That's how we find out what we are made of.

Then, too, there was the take of cartoon characters Calvin and Hobbes (Calvin's sometimes stuffed tiger).

Said Calvin in one strip, "I wonder why man was put on earth. What's our purpose? Why are we here?" Answered Hobbes, **"Tiger food!"**

Travel is a wonderful means of jumping into life, absorbing it, broadening your experience of it. The additional benefit of travel is that you learn something of yourself as you view others through the lens of your own life experience. The South African writer, Laurens Van Der Post, in *Venture to the Interior* (I commend his writing to you, strongly), says, **"A voyage to a destination, wherever it may be, is also a voyage inside oneself; even as a cyclone carries along with it the centre in which it must ultimately come to rest."**

All experience—the good and the bad—gives you something to work with, and, as Anais Nin suggests, **"Life shrinks or expands in proportion to one's courage."** Courage, of course, having less to do with fear and more to do with how you respond to fear. Anyone who says he is never fearful is either a liar or a fool and is, in either case, not to be trusted. Reminds Isaac Asimov, **"Difficulties vanish when faced boldly."** Always deal with a problem as soon as you possibly can, the better to resolve it, one way or the other. Whichever way it comes out, you learn something useful. The old Dodger pitcher, Preacher Roe, put it this way: **"Some days you eat the bear. Some days the bear eats you."**

Essential to this process is to understand that it is just that, a *process*. It is the living that intrigues, not the goal. The ultimate goal, after all, the terminus of all this process is death. Robert Louis Stevenson put it rather succinctly: **"To travel hopefully is a better thing than to arrive; true success is to labour."** The old Latin phrase that MGM Pictures adopted as their motto serves equally: *Ars gratis artis* (**art for art's sake**). It is the doing, the learning, the living that is to be valued. What we receive for our efforts is extra. "Window dressing" was once the phrase. Icing on the cake is a bit more modern.

The point is to make what you get out of your occupation

subservient to the activity itself and how you go about it. The mythologist Joseph Campbell admonished "**Follow your bliss**," implying that whatever material needs you might have ought to follow the far more spiritual needs of our labor. Rabbi Adin Steinsaltz warns that, "**There can be no greater danger to one laboring to reach a higher spiritual and moral plane than the feeling that he has achieved it. Such feelings of self-satisfaction generally indicate a blurring of the vision of the goal itself.**" As the Zen masters have likewise taught, be unattached to the fruits of one's activity, but focus on the activity itself.

When you start something, go after it. As Goethe commands, "**What you can do or think you can, begin it—boldness has genius, power and magic in it.**" If you adopt the Zen-like unattachedness to your goals, you will not be daunted by rejection. Before Edison came to carbon as the filament for his first incandescent light bulb, he had tried over a thousand others, each time taking his failure as moving himself one step closer to success. And never sit back and wait on Lady Luck, for as baseball great Branch Rickey reminded, "**Luck is the residue of design.**" [*Curtis: I think luck is just a saying for "Things happen for a reason."*] There are thousands, if not millions, of examples of overnight successes who, when asked, will happily point to the hours of painstaking practice they put in to achieve that "quick" success. Very little, in life, is given over without sustained effort.

As you know from watching me work my way through rejection notices—any writer worth his or her salt can paper a three-bedroom, two-bath house with them—I have occasionally been disheartened, but never stopped. Still, I wish that more of my rejection slips were more like that of the famed Chinese editor, who wrote, "**We have read your manuscript with boundless delight. If we were to publish your paper, it would be impossible for us to publish any work of a lower standard. . . . And as it is unthinkable that, in the next thousand years, we shall see its equal, we are, to our regret, compelled to return**

your divine composition and beg you a thousand times to overlook our short sight and timidity." Ah, well, if you put it *that* way.

Abraham Lincoln was a man who assiduously used failure as a means to knowledge. He failed in business twice, was defeated for the state legislature, had a nervous breakdown, and lost two races for the Senate. Through it all he remained centered enough to become perhaps our greatest President. He once said, **"If I were to try to read, much less answer, all the attacks made on me, this shop might as well be closed for any other business. I do the very best I know how—the very best I can, and I mean to keep doing so until the end. If the end brings me out all right, what is said against me won't amount to anything. If the end brings me out wrong, ten angels swearing I was right would made no difference."**

In charting your life courses, don't be afraid to travel the "blue highways," the lesser known paths. You never know what you might find. **"All who wander are not** lost," reminded J. R. R. Tolkein. Discovery is a wondrous experience, one not to be missed.

It helps, in times of wandering, to keep a sound sense of humor close at hand. As pianist/humorist Victor Borge liked to say, **"Laughter is the shortest distance between two people."** Daniel Boone, when asked if he ever got lost in the woods, said, **"No, but I was bewildered once for three days!"** Return with me to Henry Ward Beecher (you remember our man of character), who said, **"A man without mirth is like a wagon without springs. He is jolted disagreeably by every pebble in the road."** Or back to Aristotle's insistence that **"Wit is educated insolence."** What teen won't respond to the call to insolence? (This reminds me—don't ask why—of that delightful little cartoon, where a lion judge is preparing to sentence a lion defendant. **"You say you were hungry? Case dismissed!"** Perspective is everything.)

Of course, one of my all time favorites came from you, Tama. When you were about two, or perhaps a little past two, we took you to a petting zoo at the local park. When a lamb butted you and knocked you to the ground, you ran over to me, mumbling, "Doggie hit me!" I loved your inventive perspective then, I love it now.

A concomitant to humor is the injunction not to take yourself too seriously. There are a few things—protecting one's children from danger, taking time for your lover, considering the state of the environment—that admit to heavy, serious thought and being. But, for most of life, it pays to keep things on the lighter side. As the popular author entitled his book, *Don't Sweat the Small Stuff (It's All Small Stuff)*. Don't forget the famous Rule Number Six, which categorically lays it out: **Don't take yourself too seriously.** (What makes that memorable is the fact that when you ask about Rules One through Five, the muffled laughter only conceals the fact that ... they don't exist. Rule Number Six is it!) Then there is the wit Brendan Gill, who once wrote, "**Not a shred of evidence exists in favor of the idea that life is serious.**" [*Curtis: I shouldn't take myself* *too serious.* That is a hard lesson for you, my son, because your natural sensitivity kicks in mighty quickly. But I think you will learn this lesson, because you want to.]

Will there be those who would try to keep you from being happy? Absolutely. There are plenty of insecure, jealous people who will try and intrude upon your lives with their petty, small selves. Take the advice of Mark Twain (always good in a pinch): **"Keep away from people who try to belittle your ambitions. Small people always do that, but the really great make you feel that you, too, can somehow become great."**

THE LAST WORD, REALLY

So *live* your lives. Wallow in your lives. You own your lives, so jump in, feet first, and grasp your lives with both arms. Don't come to your maturity with rues and regrets about what might have been. Go ahead, make some mistakes, gain the wisdom of those mistakes, and go forward once again with élan and enthusiasm. Spend your days with relish . . . and mustard and catsup and any other condiment you choose. But spend them well and spend them happily, for days are life's little microcosms, adding up in their passion or in their stultification. It's your choice. I leave you with Jack London's pithy pitch for investing every bit of yourself for every day of your life: "**I would rather be ashes than dust! I would rather that my spark should burn out in a brilliant blaze than it should be stifled by dry rot. I would rather be a superb meteor, every atom of me in magnificent glow, than a sleepy and permanent planet. The proper function of man is to live, not to exist. I shall not waste my days in trying to prolong them. I shall use my time.**"

So please, make good use of the wisdom I have collected here for you. Be meteors and glow. Spend your days—and, thus, your lives—wisely. Travel slowly, but hopefully. Do not consent to bullying in any shape or form. Above all, please, do not settle for mere existence. Actively seek peace and harmony (with just a little tension in there to keep it all going, to keep it all worthy). Laugh! Dance! Love! Wallow! Live!

AND YOU CAN QUOTE
ME ON THAT

As you have seen herein, collecting quotes is a powerfully motivating force in my life. That penchant speaks to the power of the well-chosen word or quip. The power of the simplest phrase can change a life. At the very least, it offers fresh perspectives, new viewpoints.

You can see that in Eleanor Roosevelt's most empowering admonition to disregard those hurtful pricks from others, or in Alice Walker's pithy suggestion to remain open to—or even invite in—serendipity.

Throughout my life—in my work and in everyday

dealings—I have always looked for just the right word, just the right quote to punch up conversational opportunities. Here are those of my own that I employ most often.

You know the most typical greeting there is. "How are you?" Or, in Spanish, as I am working to learn, "?Que tal?" And, no, you don't answer, "About six feet" to the latter. That also means, "How's it going?" The usual, most mundane response is, "Fine." Or, "Okay." In the past, I liked, "If I were a little bit better, I'd be hard to live with." Which would always get the startled look, then smile, at the unexpected twist. Lately, though, I've stepped it up a notch (or two) with, "I'm as good as a coyote during spring lambing!" Now, that one really gets a lively response. Most folk are delighted by the stark image that creates, and some, like my girlfriend, Terry, have a hard time with its grizzly nature. You have to see it as cartoon-like to fully appreciate it.

I have a lot of fun with the word "consultant." When I see my neighbor Ayal walking his huge Himalayan pooches,

I always ask him how his consultants are faring. It's the same with other dog walkers, or even to people with their young children. "How are your consultants today?" always elicits broad smiles as they see their charges in a slightly different light.

I am an avid tennis player. If you play the game, you know that the damned net gets in the way . . . a lot. Hence, my assessment, "The Lord giveth and the net taketh away." At bat, in our adult baseball league—hardball, not softball—I always ask the pitcher, "You got a hanging slider you need to work on?" Which usually gets a laugh, and occasionally, that hanging slider that I can actually hit. I am also fond of promoting the idea that baseball is, at its essence, a very primal game: "It's like you have two cavemen," I declaim. "One's got a rock and one's got a wooden club. Let's see who's better!" The very essence of competition.

When I invite friends over for dinner—I love to cook, and have a sufficient wine cellar that will improve whatever I come up with immensely—they invariably inquire what they can bring to the party. My reply, usually, is: "Wit, charm and appetite. Or, at least, the best two of the three."

I do have a few life hacks that are designed to improve my life, and any others who find wisdom in my words. One refers to the dangerously particulate-laden air that used to hang hazily over Los Angeles like Harry Potter's Cloak of Invisibility: "Never breathe air you can see." Another is, simply, an approach to life that keeps me open to wallowing in life, to taking it all as it comes: "Something will happen." As in, when it happens, I can deal with it, but until it does, I'm not going to worry about it. As in, take life as it really happens.

I'd like to finish here with a few lines—a verse and a chorus—from a song I recently wrote for Terry, one that urges listeners to grab on to life. "Life is an 'iffy' job, a 'maybe' at its best. Go for the gold my friend, take up a mighty quest. / Grab on, life's a short ol' time, grab on, it's here right now. Grab on, let's hunker down, get all life's gusto now."

In the end—and this is the end—the beauty of a great quote is that it is a distillation of a great idea, one that gets to the very essence of the idea. That is, ultimately, the power of language, the power of ideas.

SUGGESTED READINGS

Abbott, Lyman, *Henry Ward Beecher*

Bierce, Ambrose, *The Devil's Dictionary*

Bowen, Catherine Drinker, *Yankee From Olympus* (Oliver Wendell Holmes Jr.)

Dass, Baba Ram, *Be Here Now*

Cleaver, Eldrige, *Soul on Ice*

Dalai Lama, *Ethics for a New Millennium*

Dillard, Annie, *The Writing Life*

Frankl, Viktor E., *Recollections*

Frankl, Viktor E., *Man's Search for Meaning*

Halsey, Admiral William F. USN, "The Quiet Hours" (film)

Haruf, Kent, *Plainsong*

Heinlein, Robert, *Stranger in a Strange Land*

Heinlein, Robert, *The Notebooks of Lazarus Long*

Hemingway, Ernest, *Old Man and the Sea*

Hesse, Herman, *Siddartha*

Kingsolver, Barbara, *Prodigal Summer*

Koestler, Arthur, *Darkness at Noon*

Le Guin, Ursula K. (translator), *Tao Te Ching*

Lindburgh, Anne Morrow, *Gift from the Sea*

McDonald, Roger, *Mr. Darwin's Shooter*

Mill, John Stuart, *On Liberty*

Mitchell, Stephen (translator), *Tao Te Ching*

Montaigne, *The Complete Essays*

Reynolds, Sheri, *A Gracious Plenty*

Rilke, Rainer Maria, *The Selected Poems of Rainer Maria Rilke*

Saroyan, William, *The Human Comedy*

Singer, Isaac Beshevis, *Collected Stories*

Stone, Irving, *Agony and the Ecstasy*

Thoreau, David, *Walden*

Van Der Post, Laurens *Venture to the Interior*

Walker, Alice, *The Color Purple*

Walker, Alice, *The Temple of My Familiar*

Wilder, Thornton, *Our Town* (play)

Yutang, Lin, *The Importance of Living*

THE AUTHOR

By nature a philosopher, Richard Paul Hinkle has written newspaper columns or a blog on philosophy or wine continuously since 1976 (San Francisco *Examiner*, San Francisco *Chronicle*, San Diego *Tribune*, Santa Rosa *Press Democrat*, *Pacific Sun*.) For ten years he wrote "A Mind at Large" for the New York *Times*-owned *Press Democrat*. He is also the author of nine wine books (his two *Beyond the Grapes* books won him the Wine Literary Award).

In 1976 Mr. Hinkle helped found the international wine publication, *The Wine Spectator*. He has also hosted a wine tasting radio talk show and wrote the California, Oregon and Washington chapters for the *Larousse Encyclopedia of Wine*. He scripted the video "Wines of a Place," narrated by the late Raymond Burr. ("When he was alive," says Hinkle. "It was easier that way!") After assaying roles as actor and director in community theatre, he appeared as the Warris Family lawyer in Lawrence Kasden's feature film "Mumford."

A pilot who has flown a two-place Cessna across the country twice, Mr. Hinkle also satisfied a lifelong goal by building his own home, from foundation to roof. A former crisis counselor, fireman and deputy sheriff who has taught self-esteem seminars (he also spent an all-too-short season pitching in the Cincinnati Reds organization), Hinkle lives in California's winegrowing Sonoma County. "The great advantage of being a writer," he says, "is that I was always been able to make the time to be home to read with my twins when they got home from school, hang out with them, and—this is the most fun—coach their soccer, softball, baseball and basketball teams! The three of us even played on the same indoor soccer team once."

A true baseball nut, Hinkle has a pitching machine/ batting cage in his backyard. There's a half-court basketball setup, with an NBA goal, as well. Tennis and hiking take up what little time is left when he's not writing his blog, "A Mind at Large." That can be found Tuesdays and Fridays at richardpaulhinkle.wordpress.com.

Printed in the United States
by Baker & Taylor Publisher Services